Northern Light

New Writing 2014–15

Edited by
Elsa Bouet & Tara Thomson

Volume 6

A Collection of Work from the Text & Context
and Creative Writing Courses at the
Scottish Universities' International Summer School

Northern Light: New Writing 2014–15

First published in Great Britain, 2015
by the Scottish Universities' International Summer School
21 Buccleuch Place
Edinburgh EH8 9LN
Scotland (UK)
www.suiss.ed.ac.uk

ISBN 0-9552446-5-X 978-0-9552446-5-0

Editors: Elsa Bouet and Tara Thomson.
Production Editor: Lauren Pope.
Editorial Board: Defne Cizakca, Ruth Gilligan, Russell Jones, Josianne Mamo and Hande Zapsu-Watt.

Typesetting by Kamillea Aghtan.
Cover: "See" by Line Henriksen.

Scottish Universities' International Summer School

Contents

Foreword

Northern Light has been published biennially since 2005 as a collection of the most accomplished and innovative works written as part of the Scottish Universities' International Summer School's Creative Writing course. The central theme of this sixth volume is 'Connections': the writing explores the multiple barriers that protagonists face in their attempts to create meaningful interactions with others, the difficulty of grounding themselves in space and time, but also the significance of accepting and living with one's self. These pieces move from the bitterness of failing to make connections, to expressing joy and wonder, but all express the strong human desire to form meaningful, long lasting bonds.

2015 saw the launch of our new course 'Contemporary British and Irish Theatre and Performance', so we are really pleased that this edition of *Northern Light* includes two short plays. Taylor Beidler's play presents the ways in which generational conflicts create distance between members of a family by imagining what they would say to one another should they all meet being the same age. Sean Larney's play 'Germans and Jaffa Cakes' satirises the ways stereotypes lead to cultural discrimination.

The poetry in this volume voices the difficulty to make real connections. In Jackson Burgess' poem 'Bar', drugs and alcohol distort the ability to see people or memories for what they are, creating instead illusory, hazy connections. 'Hide and Seek', by Samiya Akhtar, expresses the despair of losing someone, leaving the self disconnected from its environment, others and reality. The fast pace of Michelle Nicolaou's performance poetry accentuates the cultural and social divisions created by borders which segregate the island of Cyprus while mirroring the desire to rapidly reach reconciliation and peace. Rosa Schwenger's 'Rosa Hits Enter at a lot of Random Places' recounts her experiences at SUISS and links the friendships she formed to the literature she read on the course.

The prose works included contend with the complexity of connection, and coming to terms with difference. In Laura Tomich's short story 'Echolocation', a couple and their mutual friends reminisce over their past, while discussing the best ways to salvage a flooded flat. The protagonists move from being helpful and diplomatic to being irritated. The work done on the house mirrors the patience it can take to maintain friendships. In Emily Rogers' 'Lost Mountain, Michigan', a narrator, who travels in the mountains, struggles to interact with and make their presence known to locals and other tourists. In Anwesha Chattopadhyay's 'Stick on Indians', learning English allows the characters to deceive one another but also to empower themselves. While the couple's relationship is broken by extramarital gay affairs, the piece ultimately purports forgiveness and the acceptance of sexual difference.

All the works in *Northern Light* convey the complexities of human interaction, the pain that we can cause each other, the superficial ways in which we attempt to create meaningful relationships, and the way language itself can corrupt the messages we are trying to convey. The language of these pieces is at times complex, at times simple, brutal or poetic, but demonstrates how these exciting new writers have crafted their pieces to express the array of ways in which we make connections, successfully or not.

This volume beautifully reflects the spirit of SUISS, which was founded as a non-profit organisation by Professor David Daiches in 1947, in the wake of the Second World War. The school invites students, writers and academics from all over the world to form connections through their love of literature, irrespective of national, religious, or cultural differences.

Dr Elsa Bouet & Dr Tara Thomson
Edinburgh, November 2015

Rosa Schwenger

Rosa Hits Enter at a Lot
of Random Places

Disclaimer: All mistakes are done on purpose, obviously.
All misplaced, superfluous or lost commas are my intention.
All weirdly worded ideas are exactly what they are supposed to be.
Everything is on purpose when the purpose is to be

thrown into the cold grey weather waters
not knowing what to make of anything.
Waves of clouds clashing, whirls of winds dashing
at the periphery of our expectations,
their meaning being entangled like a knot of rain, wind and trees
while gloomy buildings watch all of our cautious steps through the seas.
And if not now then at the end we
will have fought through this jungle of modern isms and survived,
if we all follow the same threads or not.
A physical journey posed Arthur's Seat
and from up there
the two-week future mysteries of an unknown world unfolded in front
of us
and

the excitement is palpable
(who is he even?),
you can feel the suspense in the air
(never heard of this guy, to be honest),
we saw moments of greatness not only flicker but maybe burn
(or got it trust upon us)
just shortly before lots of anger aimed at structures and codes,
though not at the play at hand,
and then
the lighting of the rainbow coloured ceilings, walls,
diverse and overflowing as

all the colours of the voices of Dublin
we tried to understand.
And yes, you can watch your language
when what's said is so vivid that it doesn't matter
which sense makes sense
at a time

is space, space is time
when chaotic confusion reached its peak
with elusive allusive Eliot.
HURRY UP PLEASE TIME FLIES SO FUCKING FAST
when you're having fun-
damental thoughts and stuff.
We have no idea what we're doing
but surely some revelation is at hand
(not to use the word with E).
Instead of inhabiting a waste land
we danced in a stuffed hall
shapeless formless
but unparalysed and with

rhythm and direction
in not one but many voices which led us around the intangible centre of
trauma.
Our plunging was more of a stumbling
search for the clearest sound, the sharpest memory.
We will buy this heap of broken flowers ourselves
paying with coins that are more confusing than any stream of semi-
conscious ideas could ever be.
When opening this door to prose experiments
In the literary middle – literally the middle – of our journey

we yearn for poetry even though we may not confess it, so
make me king as we march towards a
new wor(l)d order
in India. But this could be anywhere, really
where unknown people meet people they know even less
and politics and fear do the talking.
Prepared like this we visited the parliament
but exhaustion often surpasses political ambitions as we

slouch towards the edge of the end of modernism.
In soft entropy and gyre-ish shapes
we examined the terrible beauty of
words, but also trees and grassy patches,
greyscale mazes and empty melting landscapes
in colours which shine with an absence of brightness

so that you don't know if to say
good morning, midnighters,
or good day, children of the light.
I AM NOT your window to a reality normal people can't see,
I AM NOT the truth behind.
I am the total distortion of time space meaning

of `when have I eaten showered talked to somebody last?'
of being unpleasantly surprised to still be alive but
what to do what to do
what ever is there to do.
I tried to measure out the evenings mornings afternoons
but what means measuring
what means -
It is not that I do not want to be happy
but I cannot remember what *wanting* means, or *happy* for that matter;
emotions are not even up for debate when they become the most foreign
words of all.
I would gladly set these words on fire
and all my other ones
and those I haven't written yet
if this could keep the imminent permanent constantly calling
waves of sticky black tar at bay
which suffocate me, and no matter how hard I try to breath I will drown

anyway.
Writing this today I cannot know what tomorrow might bring
but neither did Orwell nor Huxley and did they let this stop them?
This is just to say:
we will fare one another well
(whatever that means, words are so weird, have you ever looked at
them?)
and then will be catapulted into a future of undefined dimensions
and –isms yet to be explored.

ROSA SCHWENGER attended SUISS in 2015. At home, she is currently completing her
BA in British and American Studies at the University of Mannheim, Germany, and plans
to continue her studies of literature at the Masters level. She writes fiction, poetry and
passive-aggressive essays.

Taylor Beidler

Life Could Be a Dream
A Ten-Minute Play By:
Taylor Beidler

<u>Cast of Characters:</u>
<u>Ruth</u>
<u>Rhonda</u>-her daughter
<u>Rachel</u>-*her* daughter

<u>Time and Place:</u>
Respective kitchens during respective birthday parties.

(*Lights up. Each woman enters her respective
kitchen, rushing so as not to keep guests waiting
for the cake. These three women begin icing the
same style cake with the same amount of hurried
finesse. Ruth is wearing a starched A-line skirt,
frilled apron, hair in neat curls. Rhonda is
wearing a frilly purple shirt, black pants with a
wide belt buckle, hair in a sprayed updo. Rachel
is wearing a wrap dress, paisley apron, hair flat-
ironed and shoulder length.*)

RUTH/RHONDA/RACHEL: (*smearing the icing over the
cake*) Shit.

(*beat. Moment of suspicion. Women continue icing,
this time frantic.*)

RUTH/RHONDA/RACHEL: (*smearing yet more icing*) Oh,
for crying out loud.

(*beat. Women stand frozen.*)

RACHEL: Hello?

RUTH: Hello?

RHONDA: Who is this?

RACHEL: I should be asking you the same thing.

RHONDA: That's funny.

RUTH: Funny?

RHONDA: You sound familiar.

RACHEL: Familiar?

RUTH: Do I know you?

RHONDA: Damned if I know.

RACHEL: Huh.

(*They continue icing. They each taste the icing off
their pinky fingers.*)

RUTH/RHONDA/RACHEL: Scrumptious.

(*The women have finished icing the cake. They wipe
their hands off in relief. Beat.*)

RACHEL: Do I know you?

RUTH: Damned if I know.

RACHEL: That's funny.

RHONDA: Funny?

RACHEL: My grandmother always says that. My mother, too.

RUTH/RHONDA: Huh.

(The women pick up their cakes and are about to exit to their respective living rooms. They pause. Turn around.)

RUTH/RHONDA/RACHEL: Who are you?

RUTH: Ruth.

RHONDA: Rhonda.

RACHEL: Rachel.

RUTH/RHONDA/RACHEL: Oh my god.

RHONDA: Mom?

RACHEL: Grandma?

RUTH: Oh my god.

RACHEL: How old are you?

RUTH: Thirty-three.

RHONDA: Thirty-three.

RACHEL: Oh my god.

(beat. They set down their cakes. They take another pinky-full of icing.)

RUTH/RHONDA/RACHEL: Scrumptious. *(They smile.)*

RUTH: Am I mad? I must be dreaming.

RHONDA: Well, if you're dreaming then I'm downright hallucinating.

RUTH: I don't quite know what to say.

RHONDA: I'm feeling rather giddy.

RACHEL: What do we do? What does one say? If you're my mother and you're my grandmother and we're all the same age, what do we talk about?

(beat)
RUTH/RHONDA: Sex.
RACHEL: Naturally.
RHONDA: *(to Ruth)* We've never spoken about this before.
RUTH: *(to Rachel) We've* never spoken!
RACHEL: Ok, ok, let me ask you two a question: at what point did sex become predictable? How long were you married before sex became manual? These days I have as much excitement during sex as I do burping little Charlie.
RHONDA: Well, I think it comes down to spontaneity. For the past year, your father has taken it upon himself to dress up. Why, just last week, he showed up wearing nothing but a pink feather boa!
RACHEL: A pink feather—I wore that for Halloween when I was eight!
RHONDA: Well, how am I supposed to know? You're only two.
RUTH: I think that's downright silly. Sex isn't a slumber party, it's far more intimate. I for one take comfort in the reliability of sex, it's something I can depend on.
RHONDA: That boa's become pretty reliable, doesn't mean I want to depend on it! *(Rachel giggles.)*
RUTH: Don't be fresh. I'm throwing you a birthday party right now, you ought to be more grateful. In fact, you're currently in the living room singing Shirley Temple numbers for the family. They simply adore you, you know. You've got your pink taffeta dress on, it's a swell party; don't you remember?
RHONDA: Of course, I hated that dress, the collar would give me a rash around my neck.

RACHEL: You would sing Shirley Temple?

RUTH: Oh sure, your mother has this whole routine set up in a little sailor hat, too. (*sings*) "On the good ship, lollipop..."

RUTH/RACHEL: (*singing together*) "...it's a sweet trip to the candy shop where the bon-bon's play on the sunny beach of peppermint bay."

RACHEL: I can't believe you sang this, Mom! I feel like there's so much I never learned about you.

RUTH: Learned? She's right here!

RHONDA: Sweetheart, there's a reason you're not dancing out there for your birthday party: to grandparents, those routines never grow old, even if you do.

RUTH: Well, I hardly think that's true.

RHONDA: Mom, I wore that sailor cap on my graduation day.

RUTH: Well, I guess we can't do anything about that now.

RACHEL: I suppose so.

RUTH: So, Rachel, whose birthday are you celebrating?

RACHEL: Mom's, actually.

RHONDA: How about that? I must be pretty damn near over the hill by then!

RACHEL: It's your 50th.

RUTH: Oh, why now, that's not so old. I think 50's quite an accomplishment!

RACHEL: Yeah, I thought so, too.

RHONDA: Don't worry, Mom. Middle-age suits you just fine. Can't guarantee the same for me!

(*Waits for Rachel to respond. Beat. They return to their respective cakes.*)

RACHEL: *(finally)* You know, that's an interesting point you bring up. Does this change anything for us? When we walk back to see our families, will we remember any part of this, or is this just some sort of collective unconscious?
RHONDA: I'm not sure.
RUTH: Does that matter?
RACHEL: Maybe not. It's just...
RUTH: What, dear?
RACHEL: Nothing.
RHONDA: It's okay, go ahead, what have we got to lose?
RACHEL: That's exactly it. What if this, whatever this is, gives us the power to change the past?
RUTH: I suppose that depends on what you would like to change.
RHONDA: There's no harm in trying.
RUTH: Do you have something in mind?
RACHEL: *(pause)* Are you happy?
RHONDA: What do you mean?
RACHEL: Right now. At 33. Icing your cake. Hosting your party. Could you honestly look at me and tell me you're happy?
RUTH: Well, I like to think I'm very grateful for everything I have, Henry and I get along fine and I like to think I'm a good mother and-
RHONDA: *(cutting RUTH off)* No.
RUTH: What's that?
RHONDA: *(with increased fervor)* You're right. I'm not. I'm not happy. I want to be. I pretend to be. But I don't feel like enough. I love you, Rachel-pie, and you too, Ma, but sometimes I feel guilty for feeling this way and I...I can't breathe.

RUTH: Oh, come now, that's normal. You have your moods now as a child. Just let them pass.

RACHEL: No, Grandma, they won't pass.

RHONDA: I don't know if the person I want to be and the person I'm meant to be are two entirely different people and I'm not sure if I've become either of them. I knew no matter how many times you had me sing I was never going to be Shirley Temple, and no matter how many times I ice these damn cakes I'm never going to play the perfect hostess.

RACHEL: I always loved our parties, Mom.

RHONDA: I'll send you away the day after our parties, do you remember? You'll go to Grandma's while I clean up the house? But I never do. Clean. The house at least. I take baths, and the water feels so accommodating. I submerge. I hold my breath for ten seconds, twenty seconds, and by thirty seconds there's this voice that starts to whisper, "Just go. It's okay. You've done enough. You can go now. Leave." Forty seconds. All I want is this voice in my head to keep talking, and by fifty seconds it starts to scream at me, and my lungs are wrung dry and my face feels windburnt and I can't hold it any longer. I give up. I breathe. Like I'm supposed to. *(pause.)* I've never told that to anyone before. Didn't know I had it in me.

RUTH: Oh, my...

RHONDA: Rachel?

RACHEL: Yes, Mom?

RHONDA: Am I there at your birthday party?

RACHEL: *(pause)* No, Mom.

RHONDA: Somehow I knew that.

RUTH: I'm there, though. I have this feeling like

I'm there.

RACHEL: Yes, Grandma, you're here. You're sitting in an armchair, in the corner. Everyone comes over to kiss your cheeks.

RUTH: So this party I'm attending, it's--

RACHEL: An anniversary.

RHONDA: Of what would have been my 50th.

(pause.)

RUTH: What do we do now?

RACHEL: What can we do now?

RHONDA: "On the good ship, lollipop..."

RACHEL: I love you, Mom.

RHONDA: I love you, Rachel-pie.

RUTH: This has to change things. I refuse to believe that we can talk like this and go back feeling powerless. We'll just have to keep baking cakes is all. Make sure we're all accounted for. That's the ticket!

RHONDA: (smiles weakly) Sure thing, Mom.

RACHEL: I'm looking forward to it.

(pause. They have finished icing the cake.)

RUTH: Well, onwards I suppose!

RACHEL: Yes, everyone will be wondering where we are.

RHONDA: Yes, they must be. Well, then...

RUTH: I don't know what to say again.

RACHEL: Until next time.

RHONDA: Until then.

RUTH: So long, ladies. I expect to see you soon.

(she exits)

RACHEL: Mom?

RHONDA: Yes, sweetheart.

RACHEL: Seventeen years from now, from your now,

I'm going to call you and tell you I'm on my way
home for your 49ᵗʰ birthday party. I'll ask you how
you are. Mom, whatever you do, don't say "fine." I
won't believe it. I can't.

RHONDA: I'll do my best.

RACHEL: We have to go back now.

RHONDA: Yes.

RACHEL: I wish you were here.

RHONDA: Maybe now I will be.

RACHEL: *(smiles weakly)* Of course.

RHONDA: One more thing.

RACHEL: Yeah?

RHONDA: Are you happy? No one asked you. I don't
think I've ever asked you.

RACHEL: I've got some ups and downs, obviously,
but...yeah. I think I am.

RHONDA: I have a feeling I'll remember that.

RACHEL: Bye, Mom.

RHONDA: Goodbye, Rachel-pie. Until next time.

*(The two women pick up their cakes, take one last
moment, turn around, and exit upstage.)*

TAYLOR BEIDLER is in her third year pursuing her BFA in Theater Arts from Boston University. Taylor focuses much of her studies on playwriting and dramaturgy. She hopes to continue encouraging dynamic female voices in the theater today, through writing of her own and through the pursuit of literary management.

Jackson Burgess

Bar

In the end it wasn't about love, it was about
sharing saliva on pint glasses and beneath
sheets. We all picked poison over passion and hoped
we could summon some meaning out of it—
but the smug bartender just kept pouring shots
and the only spirits present were those behind the bar.
I stepped outside and met a homeless couple,
starved, dressed in shopping bags, who told me
about the bone cathedral in their hometown.
I couldn't tell what drugs they were on
but I wanted some. The woman's eyes grew bigger
as she described the pews lined with femurs,
the pulpit made of skulls, and when I went back in
to tell my friends, no one believed me.
So we drank, some of us to forget, others to remember
the days before prescriptions and addictions,
when the sun and streets and trees were enough.
But it's never enough. All we have at the end
of the night are grainy memories of the floor
and how it stuck to our soles, like it didn't want us
to leave, like it wanted to hold us
until time stripped us to bone.

Escape Plan

Whenever I see planes cruising through the sky I jump in
and imagine looking downward at my house,
where I'm going, where I've been, what I'm running from,
who's chasing me. It's usually a girl whose tongue
I've accidentally bitten off, and she usually has needles
or knives, something sharp—never blunt, never as easy
and senseless as a hammer or brick, because
that's not how heartache works. I thought I was getting better
at amputations, but there's no such thing as a clean break
or a smooth getaway, which is why every attempt at escape
via flight ends in catastrophe: the man sitting next to you
has rabies, you fly into a cloud made of ice,
your brain suddenly ingests itself, and still you try,
you practice pillow talk and sweet nothings, you go through
all the motions, knowing it will end, knowing someone
somewhere will have you placed on a bed of nails
and lay themselves on top of you, delicately,
stroking your face as they push and push.

JACKSON BURGESS is the author of Pocket Full of Glass, winner of the 2014 Clockwise Chapbook Competition (forthcoming, *Tebot Bach*). He is currently pursuing dual MFAs in Poetry and Fiction at the Iowa Writers' Workshop as a Truman Capote Fellow. (jacksonburgess.com)

Line Henriksen

Cat's Lunch

"Cat got your tongue?"

"…"

"Was it the tabby one, with the big grin and just one eye? Yeah, something should be done about that one. Last week, it caught Mrs. Faulkner's eye! If only people were a little more careful with where they put their body parts, we wouldn't be having all this trouble, would we? I mean, eyes alone tend to wander if you're not quick. And I hear young Johnson lost a head and a heart last night."

"*Hrunt!*"

"You know, without a tongue, you kinda sound like a pig. But there's the cat! Up there, in that tree! It seems good-natured enough, but it's got quite a few teeth. Better treat it with respect, I guess."

"*Hrunt-rrunt.*"

"Here, kitty kitty. Nice kitty. Good kitty."

"How kind of you to say!"

"Oh! It's found a way to work your tongue. And Mrs. Faulkner's eye!"

"I can't take all the credit for that. It's partly due to Mr. Hanson's deft fingers."

"You stole the tailor's hand!"

"I admit, I bit the hand that fed me. But it was a fair exchange, I swear! He's got a pest problem, the tailor, and I've always had quite the flair for mouse catching –"

"It really does sound like you now …"

"*Hrunt-hrunt.*"

" - he'll be happy to have acquired such a skilled paw, I'm sure. And he can still sew with his right hand."

"Yeah, so, are you gonna give this one his tongue back?"

"I'm afraid not, I've become quite attached to it. But don't worry: I've kept the old one."

"You did WHAT?"

"*Squeeeel!*"

"Now, be kind. He does sound an awful lot like a pig, doesn't he? Do you want a tongue or not?"

" … "

"I think that means 'yes'."

"Coming right up! Hre*ee* … hre*ee* … hrrre*eeeeee* …"

"Are you alright?"

"… hre*ee*-waaaiieeet-he*ee* …"

"Is it gonna …?"

"*Squeeeeeeel!*"

"Argh, seriously!"

"I do apologise."

"It hit him square in the face!"

"I did apologise!"

"It's a bloody hairball!"

"Open it."

"Ew … wait … this is not a tongue – it's young Johnson's heart!"

"Oh. So it is. My apologies. Will you throw it back here, please?"

"Hell no! This thing belongs to young Johnson! He's lost a head and a heart, and you ate it all!"

"If you keep the heart, that one there will just have to learn to speak from it. I'm keeping the tongue."

"*Hrunt-hrunt!*"

"Okay, alright, take it, then."

"Aim for the mouth … *aarh* … sanks. Now, let's see … hurre*eee* – hre*eeee* – *hreeeerr …heeeeeer*e …"

"Will you learn to aim!"

"There - a present! Open it. See what it is."

"Your old tongue …"

"Just his size, too! A few corrections and it'll fit perfectly. Now, I'll just get the needle and thread …"

"Do you keep everything in your mouth?"

"It's practical. Now, come closer … open wide … a stitch here and a stitch there and up and down and up and down … aaaaand … All done! Give it a whirl, why don't you?"

"*Meuuwe …*"

"Spoken like a true cat! Did you say pig, or fig?"

"*Mreuw …*"

"My words exactly!"

"Purrrr*reee* …?"

"Well, that depends a good deal on where you want to get to? In that direction lives a cat-eyed old lady. In that one lives a mouse-catching tailor."

"*Puurrrrree ...*"

"Hey! No licking my hands! Wait ... you going? He's going. I never really liked much of what he had to say as a person, but I have to admit, he makes quite the eloquent cat. I could think of a few others who'd make better cats than people. But wait - whatever happened to young Johnson's head?"

"Well, some meat is for sewing, some is not."

"What do you mean?"

"I was hungry."

LINE HENRIKSEN lives in the cold, dark depths of Sweden, where there is no hope and no shops open on a Sunday. Her work has appeared or is forthcoming in theEEEL by tNY.Press, freeze frame fiction, Pankhearst's *Wherever you Roam* and *The Unlikely Coulrophobia Remix*.

Visit her at www.henriksenline.wordpress.com.

Samiya Akhtar

Athazagoraphobia

There are many things I don't know but here's a fact:
at some point in our lives you will tell me my soup tastes like shit
and I will cry enough to go to sleep in a bathtub.
How lonely it is to obsess over a future yet to happen
and still make it sad.
Like staring at the stack of coffee cups on your desk
and realizing there will always be things
you will never wake up from.
How awfully convenient to suffer heartbreak,
and smoke it away by the dumpster.
Like your favourite sweater smelling like a stranger.

But here's what is true:
you have been the wind-chime smothered by the drapes,
the clock stuck at five minutes to noon, and if we could just try,
maybe we could get eleven cups of cappuccino again,
celebrate the genius of David Lynch.
Remember how we laughed about that, and what it all meant.
We bonded over "Eraserhead" and that night I went to sleep
thinking how lovely it would be to be stranded
on the top of the Ferris wheel with you,
feeling nauseated.

Sometimes, when I'm walking a busy street in Delhi,
distracting myself from thinking of every girl who's ever been afraid,
or when I see an old man on the bus in a foreign country, struggling
to make sense of the tiny scrap of paper in his hand,
I think of the summer by the fountain, the gnats in our drinks,
your flashing molars.

I think of us,
and our quest to traverse the whole country on a mere resolve,
backed by cheering friends and expired soda cans.
Who could blame us, nifty small-towners,
plucking hope from dying lanterns,
humming along to the rattling bones of strict ancestors
when winter was endurance and summer was a bull.

But here's what I wish:
I wish they spelt it out, our mothers and fathers,
concerned friends and well wishers.
I wish they told us, that despite the piling bills,
the mismatched socks hung out to dry,
there was warmth to be found
in the stabby void of morning sheets,
and things to be learnt
from the way the carpet hugged our toes,
insisted we were happy.

Hide and Seek

Most nights, I wake up clutching my heart
as if it was your palm and you were falling off a cliff.
I peek inside my nightshirt, glimpsing the hidden casket
where your Polaroid remains are stacked
like postcards to nowhere.
I pull at the lock, just in case.
I can let the burnt toast sit there for another day;
it has started to feel like home.
The coffee beans have dried up.
The apothecary table has transformed into a cemetery
where half-finished poetry is strewn like corpses.
You can try, but that soil won't see spring anytime soon.
The hospital walls have evaporated in a cloud of pink smoke
but the smell of disinfectants
still finds its way through the window crack.

The therapist tells me:
"The mind will repress things on its own."
I wait – a sad little masochist with webbed feet.
It was the third of the sixth and suddenly,
my arms were flailing in the wind,
my eyes wide enough to contain all the rain.
In the dark of the night, I stood, waiting
for a flash of lightning to guide me home
one step at a time,
and, ever since you died,
I have made every red light
I have tapped the wood twice.

SAMIYA AKHTAR is an Indian, a woman of color, an English major, a poet, and a fierce advocate of power-naps. On most days, she just wants to read good poetry and eat her weight in French-fries. She is currently working on a poetry manuscript. She lives and writes from the historical city of Lucknow.

Julie Walker

Lightning

Key kicked her feet hard, diving down further into the dark water. The bay was never particularly clear, and now at night it was blacker than ever, but that did not matter. She had a mission to fulfil.

Little eddies issued from her hands as she cut through the water, avoiding the various dark spots and sunken debris which reached for her from the depths, threatening to catch her. A flash of lightning transformed the water into a sea of white fire, the world around her thrown into binary contrasts. The brief light revealed a wickedly sharp piece of metal garbage close to her face, and Key started back. Her ponytail wafted forward with the movement, swaying in front of her eyes like unruly seaweed.

She swam carefully around the metal spike, and tried to recall what had happened to the clones before her. Some data had been relayed to her – just the basics, really – but she had little consequent memory of a shared history. There were some hazy images - a lot of water, and cold, and dark, none of which was useful information. Protocol suggested that clones were usually privy to more of their predecessors' memories, but she had been needed quickly, so she assumed they'd cut corners.

Key swam slower now, and let her thoughts slide away from questions as it got too dark to see. Instead, she focussed on her target: the ship just beneath her.

Inside what used to be the captain's cabin was a safety box which needed retrieving, no questions asked – which was why Key's agency had been contacted. She had been sent out the same night, and the mission had to be completed before sunrise, around five hours from now. Plenty of time to search an abandoned vessel. All she needed to do was find one of the entrances.

Her hands, which had been brushing ahead of her carefully, encountered a smooth metal surface – she had found the hull. She reached to turn on her helmet lights, when her comm sprang to life, emitting a burst of static in her ear.

Key's heart rate quickened – she had almost forgotten about the comm – and an unexpected sense of déjà vu swept over her, threatening to push her under. The dark seemed to grow darker for a moment.

"Are you listening to me?" the voice grated. Key switched on her control wristpad, the faint glow reflecting eerily on the ship's smooth bulk. She activated the keyboard, tapped out a Morse code response and waited.

"Thank you. As I was saying, do not activate your lights [bzzt] may set off the traps."

Key paused. There had been no mention of traps in the briefing. Or had there? *Don't lose focus*, she told herself.

She typed an affirmative, and switched off the wristpad, leaving her in darkness again.

Key thought she could feel the pressure of the water increasing, even though her suit was giving her no indication of any change. She wondered if her info display was broken, and angled herself to what she thought was the ocean floor. Squinting through the darkness, she tried to see how far down she was. A flash of lightning lit up the sky, and reflected off the massive hull of the ship, illuminating the water.

There were bodies on the seabed, swaying boredly with the current. It was hard to tell in the brief flash, but it looked like several dozen at least.

Key felt panic rising up in her chest like a bubble, then quashed it firmly.

She was a soldier. And soldiers were not rattled, not even when they were in a deep pool of water in the black of night with corpses drifting invisibly beneath them.

Her hands shook as she swam further down to find an entrance, kicking her feet and feeling her way along the side. As she tried to ignore a sudden unintelligible babble of voices on her comm, her hand ran over a handle, and Key realised she was touching a deadbolt, which marked one of the doors.

The babbling grew louder, and then faded away, leaving a silence which filled Key with an unspeakable dread. The deadbolt in her hand felt both familiar and very, very wrong.

She braced herself to push the bar aside, but her hands would not comply, and released it like she had been shocked. Right on cue, the commander barked in her ear.

"Well? Are you inside yet?" In the background, she could hear the low murmur starting again.

She tapped a response.

"The door is booby-trapped? How do you know?"

Key answered.

"A feeling?" the buzzing in the background got more excited. "Well, that's unscientific. But better safe than sorry, I suppose. Keep looking!"

She gave a short affirmative, and swam deeper. She was glad about the underwater comms; it was nice to hear human voices down here. It certainly dissipated the feeling that she was the last living creature in the world.

She found another door, with a similar deadbolt, only this one was already open, and the hole into the ship felt colder and blacker than the water around it. The lock was twisted and odd under her hands. She wondered why a ship would need doors with bolts on the outside. It seemed illogical.

She took a large breath of the canned air in her oxygen tank, and grabbed hold of the doorframe. And ignoring the hammering of her less than 36-hour-old heart, Key reached into the ship to pull herself forward. Her glove touched the inner wall. Click.

The explosion rocked the entire world. Key was sinking through the water, down towards the bodies. A flash of lightning –

A wide swath of night-blackened blood, tracing Key's progress from the ship's door and the trap to the floor of the ocean –

A glimpse at the pile of bodies, all with her uniform, all with her face, their unblinking disappointed eyes watching her –

A crackling on her miraculously still-intact comm –

"Better than last time – "

"Almost twice as long – "

"Better next time – "

The storm moved on, and the bay was dark again.

J.K. WALKER lives in Vienna, Austria with the two obligatory cats. She holds a BA in Cultural Anthropology, and will be finishing her MA in Literature any day now, promise. She writes short stories and longer ones, TV scripts, game scripts and to do lists.

Cara Fromm

Relativity (Time Dilation)

They tell us that the tickertape will wait
for our return. Farewells that stretch for days
all end with switching lights off, saying, amazed,
"I'm leaving at the speed of *that*." The date
arrives and we depart, our calendars
in hand. On Earth, it will be many years
until our shuttle lands, but way up here,
past rusted Mars, time slows. We travel far—
our view's a blur. Communication drops
one day—machines start spitting fire—and so
we sit, play cards, and ration food. We grow—
not old, but tired—then turn around. We stop
at home to see the friends we know have aged,
but we're too late: our planet's just a grave.

Metropolis

At first, you see it while dissecting frogs
in science class: the bumps along your skin,
though far less green, are quite amphibian.
You middle school marvel, all zits and UGGs
and bras that look and fit like slingshots, clogged
pores you combat with face wash (you can't win),
and chipping, bitten nails—you're alien,
as slime-encrusted as the frogs' pinned legs.
Yet you are city more than mutant teen,
with trellised steel beams wrapped around your teeth
and dueling voices always in your head.
Your shoes are zoned for new growth, and there's been
a lot of late. Skeletal highways, lithe,
stretch skyward, for the best may be ahead.

CARA FROMM is in her third year at Northwestern University in Evanston, Illinois, where she studies Creative Writing and Psychology. Though prone to getting lost, she found her way back home from SUISS 2015 and is now tasked with raising two houseplants and remembering where she left her keys.

Jane Threefoot

Museum Piece

shore leave
coming soon   rest   best pleasure planet   can't wait
shooting through   space   hug light-limit   be there no time soon

call comes
wreckage damn   interference   protocols
stop   check tech shouldn't be   virgin system?

scans show
foil streamers metal tumors metal toothpick struts   terran make?
aboard   history   ancient   artefact desiccate   bodies

settlers left
long ago   slow to go   pilgrims froze   sleep   wait
died alone   failure break   finalize   new home

        we forgot them.

couldn't   home
               far
               broken
                        slow
couldn't call
      radio
              delay
              blocked
      silence
couldn't   fix
     asleep
    no   parts
    dying dead

message back
  sure   instantaneous
relate surprise   exploration dangerous

lost souls
  to rest

so glad
live now   modern tech
                                reliable
        light-hugger
        ansible
won't
        lost
        can't affect ....

                ....

        ....

[*end recording*]

Jane Threefoot is a senior at Carnegie Mellon University double-majoring in Electrical and Computer Engineering and Creative Writing. She attended suiss's Creative Writing course in 2014.

Laura Moreira Tomich

Echolocation

A frustrated shout rattles dust down from the ceiling fan. I sneeze. I had been staring at the meandering fixture since the last landscape/gutter/siding expert had left. The house has been dissolving around us since we made the downpayment. Monday the ceiling in the add-on crumbled into a chalky heap on top of the fruit basket. The roof is insufficiently pitched, apparently. We only just put it back together. Then Hurricane Marnie came through.

"How was work?" I call out.

"Shit. Something's wrong," Bill replies.

"Where?"

"Fuck."

"Bill, where are you?" I don't feel like echolocating my husband. Left to his own devices he'll keep on yammering like I'm standing right there next to him. Well, louder.

"How the fuck did you miss this?"

"Bill."

"Downstairs. Shit. I think the carpet's shot."

The basement/ground floor of our split-level looks normal. Grey carpeting is tucked under the shiny, custom bookshelves that don't quite fit the space. They were Stan's housewarming gift. The new flatscreen is on its stand with the Blu-ray and VCR. The sofa, chairs and Bill's tenth desk are still arranged in neat clusters.

Bill gestures to the books, "We need to get these out of here."

He's in his undershirt in the middle of the room, his new slacks rolled up around his knees. His shirt, shoes, and socks are in a heap by the door. His feet squirsh against the carpet as he moves towards me. He has bandaids where his toenails should be.

"There's water everywhere. Take off your socks. Didn't you get the phone? I need to call Stan."

"Where's yours phone?" I reply, contorting to tear off my nylons.

"Dead."

"You didn't grab dinner on the way home, then?"

"Get the phone, please? And take some books."

I leave the books at the kitchen door. The last time we'd used the landline had been after dinner last week, with that speaker? Bill had been putting glasses away above the stove. Yes, the handset is tucked in behind the first row of tall stems. I clamber down off the counter and take it to Bill.

"Great." He says dialing "Could you keep on..."

He waves his forearm in a circle. I nod.

"Great... Hey man" Bill wanders outside to convince Stan to come over and help.

Bill and Stan lived together in grad school. They balanced each other out. Stan knows which end of a hammer to hold. He can catch a ball on the first try. Bill knows how to keep up to date with the electric. Stan is expansive. He fills all the gaps in the room. I used to work in his machine shop. After four months trying to function in the refrigerated, chaotic bunker he called a workspace, I was invited over to their place for the first time. Bill answered the door. The first floor was filled with all Stan's "kids" drinking cut rate beer or boxed wine and bickering about friction. Bill had a puke colored sweater-vest and the best smile. We started talking. The chicken wound up burnt. After dinner, Stan held court from the far corner of the sofa, a bottle of whiskey at his elbow. Bill wound up wedged between me and the fireplace. The conversation flowed between the two of them all night.

Before we bought this place Stan absolutely had to give it his seal of approval. Otherwise Bill refused to make the downpayment.

I squish-splat over to the shelf where Bill left off, in the middle of our old school books. I make sure that the first half of Bill's battered copy of Thompson -- front cover through page 256 -- didn't get separated from the second. The cold has started to creep up my toes. It takes around five trips to get the complete works of Marx and Engels. Each new stack goes to the right of the previous. After Bill's stuff, I move on to my own giant textbooks, and journals, that are lit up with technicolor flags. The damp chill sneaks up my metatarsals toward my ankle.

"He'll be 10 minutes," Bill interrupts my book-moving trance. He has two steaming mugs in his hands. "The river's gone back down. He'd've had to come around, otherwise."

"How's the water getting in, anyway?"

Bill shrugs. He hands me a mug. It's cider. We take a moment.

We form a two person book chain. He takes the books off the shelf and brings them to the stairs. I put them in stacks pressed against the perimeter. My feet start to thaw. Bill hands me a pile of *Nature*. I take it to the far side of the couch. Headlights flash into my eyes then abruptly cut off. I blink.

Bill opens the door to Stan saying, "Hey man, basement's flooded."

"I can tell." They hug. "Your porch is dry, though, right? Let's you and me get the heavy stuff up there. Then we can see what's what."

I'm assaulted by the smell of stale tobacco and sweat. When Stan hugs me he stuffs my face into his armpit and, with his other hand, shoves a six pack into my ear. "Hey, Devie."

"Stan." I take the beer and hand it to Bill. "Hon, why don't you put these in the fridge?"

Bill takes the beer up.

I go over to the empty bookcase nearest the door that goes out back. "We should get started."

"Better get the door first." Stan replies, hanging up his coat.

"Let's head out this way. Do you mind getting the other half?"

I open the backdoor. The buzz of the cicadas invades. On three I lead Stan up the stairs, hauling a bookcase between us.

"How's João doing?" I start making conversation.

"You'd know more than me. I think."

"It's been a while since I've had a chat with him about anything other than mirror alignment."

"Jon's futzing a lot. In lab, I mean. He said he couldn't get away tonight. But you know that. Sorry. He hasn't been home much."

The case is slippery in my hands. I pull my fingers in tighter. Stan fidgets. The case wobbles side to side. It slips slightly downwards in my grip.

Stan continues, "I'm not being fair. Am I Devie? He wants better images. For the tenure review. I'm getting jealous of his damn microscope. I don't even know. Tell me I'm being an idiot."

"I have no idea, Stan. Are you an idiot?"

We tuck the case under the eves, into the "L" where the sunroom attaches to the house.

"I don't know if you've met him, yet. Jon's got this new student. Fucking stunning."

"Chris?"

"Yeah, that's him."

"Have you met Christine?"

"Who?"

"His girlfriend. She's my student."

I go back through the door first. Bill is there waiting, "Devon, why don't I help –"

He's going to try to do heavy lifting with Stan. "I think we've got the bookcases handled, hon."

Bill gives me his "I-know-how-to-be-careful-around-Stan" look.

I try again, "I'll just clear off your desk, then. So that we can move it."

That gets me a glare.

Stan says, "Man, you mind clearing off that table, too? That way Devie and me can take it out, once we're done with the shelves."

Bill takes a pile of folders and heads towards the internal stairs.

Stan shuffles the next set of shelves away from the wall. From the opposite end of the cases he made for us, I listen to Stan lay out his anxieties: about Chris, about João not coming home at night, about the review that João has coming up at the end of the year: "What do I do, anyway? It was better when you two were in school."

My knees start to lock up as we yo-yo between the icy indoors and the warm, dry evening air. We manage to shove the last piece of furniture under the roof.

Stan breaths out, "This'll all be out here a while. If the carpet's done in."

"Don't say that out loud."

"Well Devie, I love breaking bad news to you."

I laugh. "I'll get that door open. We can make this fit in the sunroom."

Stan checks his watch.

"I told Jon I'd be home."

"Do you think he's going to be home now?"

"Shit."

"His stomach isn't going to tell him 'it's time to' leave for another few hours."

"Maybe I want to be there with dinner ready."

"Seriously?"

"Dev."

Bill comes out of the sunroom door.

"Could one of you give me a hand?" He looks both of us up and down. "What's up?"

"Rain," I answer.

"It won't rain," Stan said.

"Because rain is the only thing can happen out here at night."

Bill interrupts, "Should I just smash the TV to pieces while the two of you fight?"

"I'd feel better if we took care of this now," I answer.

"You two can work it out in the morning." Stan follows Bill down to the basement.

They each take one end of the flat screen. As he lifts, the corner catches the hem of Bill's shirt. He balances the TV in one hand while he tugs the shirt back down, covering the lighter patch of skin. The scar stretches from his left knee up and across his chest.

Stan liked to host Thanksgiving. Bill cooked. Frying the turkey is apparently not cooking. Stan would set a jumbo fryer up in the driveway. Everyone'd cluster around waiting for the bird to explode. I brought João with me that year. João – this was before he'd started to "call-me-Jon" everyone – was working with me. He and Stan really hit it off, bonding over a mutual love of solid state physics, and soccer. Bill came over to help pull the bird out. As it cleared the oil, Stan was making a point about uncertainty. He used his whole body for emphasis. The contents of the fryer spilled all over Bill.

We finish emptying the basement.

"Let's pull up the carpet before I leave. I'll be by in the morning. I'll bring bagels. And Jon."

With everything out of the way it's easy to pull the carpet up. And the padding. Everything is drenched. Bill decides to destroy the warranty on the vacuum to get as much water as he can.

We stand there with our bare feet on the rough concrete.

Bill sighs, "The hell do we do with all this?"

Stan answers, "There's nothing you can do. Just wait and see if it molds."

"Some fans might help."

I sigh, "It's going to mold no matter what we do."

"Devon."

"Fine, why don't Stan and I –"

Bill cuts in, "Why don't you get us some fans?"

"Just get all that carpet flat-ish."

I hunt down the fans. As I drag each one down I get snapshots of the boys arranging the carpeting: The two of them arguing at opposite ends, flinging water whenever they have a point to make. Then dragging the carpet to the driest side of the room trying to get it at flat as possible. Another, dryer bit of wild gesticulating. Stan going at the padding with a boxcutter while Bill fusses with the fans. I bring down the last fan. I join Stan cutting the padding into manageable pieces.

Stan leaves. The frantic energy drains out of the basement. Bill looks at the waves of carpeting.

"Any chance this is salvageable?"

We shower together. The water burns off the recalcitrant chill in our joints. I wash the dappled and puckered skin of Bill's torso. The bandaids on his toes are a wreck. They've frayed, fallen askew and, in the case of his big toes come off entirely. Some of them even have rusty patches. His nail beds, battered by his sneakers until they've given up on actual nails, are cracked in places and exposed to the scalding water.

"Need a hand?" I asked.

We finish getting ready for bed. He passes me the sculpted "fingertip" bandaids and some antiseptic cream. He takes the rest to his side of the bed. He sprawls out so that I can do his left foot.

In the morning, we will have to deal with Stan. And João. The bookcases on the porch. And the sparrows that will have decided to start a family in them.

In the morning, the doorbell will ring. I will go down in my pajamas. My feet will scrape on the basement floor. Stan and João will be at the door with an extra large bag of bagels with all the fixings.

"Food, Devon."

João will give me a kiss on each cheek and Stan will give me his bag.

We will need to work out how to get rid of the carpet and what we want to do with the basement. While Bill and I are disagreeing politely about what we want to do, Stan will point out the new hole in the sodden plaster. And the crack in the cement that the plaster had been hiding.

Laura Moreira Tomich graduated from Mount Holyoke College in 2012 with a degree in Mathematics. She lives in the Southern Tier of New York State, where she works as a freelance editor.

Forrest Williams

A Hare Hunt

We arrive at a frozen swamp.
I tromp by the frosty pines in my snowshoes.
Our beagle plows, nose to the ground, through the deep powder.
She is unfazed by the cold, and I watch as her snuffling gets louder.
She starts to bay as she chases a hare out of hiding. I don't lift my gun in
                                                                    time.
Barely a minute goes by and then the guns start pounding.
As the last shot resounds in the sharp winter air,
I curse the whole lot of them—the other hunters—especially my brother.
He always drops hares, one after another.

FORREST WILLIAMS is from Old Forge, New York. He will be graduating from Emory & Henry College in December, 2015 with a degree in English Literature. He plans to pursue an MFA in Creative Writing this coming fall.

Rachel Weber

To keep a distance

I get on an airplane
or pull a curtain open
or set a caged bird free

I light lamps to spite
the dark
Pull out lashes
to let more light in

I rip a photograph
and spread the pieces
empty the change
bucket
on the tile floor

Look for pennies
near the curb
where I last saw
your car

And sometimes,
I find
them.

Rachel Weber has been teaching English for 11 years at Sachem High School East on Long Island, New York and is a graduate student in Applied Linguistics at Columbia University.

Anwesha Chattopadhyay

Stick-on Indians

They sat next to each other for the first time on the flight to Heathrow. He let her take the window seat, so that she could watch the world she knew recede and flatten into Lego blocks as she sipped thick red tomato juice from a clear plastic cup. He sat next to her in the middle row, warm leg pressed close to hers in the tiny economy class seats, and slept through the entire journey. She could barely blink.

They weren't the kind of people who arrived in a brand new country with only a few pounds to their names and the shirts on their backs. She'd packed heavy—too heavy, some would say—filling two large American Touristers to the brim with wedding presents, *sarees* and sweets, and even mundane toiletries like toothpaste, washing powder and soap.

"You're not going to a deserted island, you know," Abhi, her brother, had sniggered. "There'll be shops there."

"Well, technically, they are *Isles*," she'd retorted, slipping just a few more books and *papads* at the bottom of her case. She knew of a woman, a distant aunt, who would line her luggage with dozens of brand new *sarees* every time she visited Kolkata from the States. She'd sell them to expats at ten times their cost price when she got home, using the profit to recoup the expense of the ticket. She herself couldn't do that, she had no head for numbers. Her husband was the programmer; that was his forte. Besides, it wasn't a very respectable thing to do.

It wasn't an arranged marriage; they'd known each other for years. First day at the Scottish Church College, she'd immediately fallen for the pale boy sitting all by himself, scratching equations on the worn teak desks with a pencil. Thin, tall, fair (So fair that they'd said that he must have had some "Anglo" blood in him) with white bones jutting awkwardly from underneath the translucent skin like lies. He'd asked her out to tea. They'd shared paper plates of street corner chowmein—grey earthworm-like noodles beneath heretic green shards of cucumber. Then he'd graduated, and they'd lost touch. She'd gone to the medical college; he'd left the state, and eventually the country. Seen other people, broken up with other people, run into each other again, and everybody had said, "Wasn't that serendipitous?"

"Why don't we get married?" he'd said to her, two sentences into their first real conversation after they'd met again. He'd peered at her steadily through expensive square framed Ray Bans, so much more stylish than the cheap Chinese wire frames he used to wear.

She'd looked back at him, the dull roar of dusty Kolkatan traffic outside filtering through the vents into the air-conditioned cafe, and somehow found herself saying, "Why don't we?"

Two months, one hasty wedding, and they were going to Scotland together.

They were both running away.

He could see that, even as they sat opposite each other in the erratically air-conditioned cafe.

They left the country together, settled in their small Edinburgh flat, put *Batik* print sheets on the mattresses and *Chanachur* in the kitchen, and called it home. They went to the part of town where they sold 69p soft drinks instead of the better £1 brands, and ate at a little Indian restaurant with stick-on white *Alpana* patterns on the floors and windows. They learnt to eat rice with forks instead of spoons.

They went on the bus tours, walked through the castle, held hands as they attempted to puzzle out the artistic merit in old plastic bags hung on the ceiling at the Museum of Modern Art. They took hundreds of photos and emailed them to their friends; shyly standing in front of centuries-old homes, where famous poets had lived, and ancient rolling green hills, where it was rumoured that fairies had. They danced at Ceilidhs, circling each other in an eerie re-enactment of the revolutions around the sacred pyre during their wedding ceremony, sampled Haggis, and argued about the respective virtues of Robert Burns and Rabindranath Tagore. They remarked upon how much *better* the buses were here, with free Wifi and no weary passengers hanging from the railing like combs of ripe yellow bananas. Everything was beautiful; pretty as a postcard. It was easy to pretend that the thing they were building together was beautiful too.

He stayed late at work a few nights a week, going to the pub outside the office. He met a beautiful man with golden hair and loch-blue eyes. Barra.

When Barra spoke the words pricked his skin like warm green grass at mid-day below Arthur's Seat.

To learn a language you have to fight in it.

She had never been great at the English tongue. Hadn't needed to be: she spoke with the scalpel, with warm blood gushing through her fingers and thin silver needles piercing pink flesh. When she used words, she preferred the Bengali tongue or the occasional Latin scientific name. But here, in this new country, she truly learnt to speak English.

They screamed at each other, accusations flying back and forth.

"*Ki hoeche?*" She asked him in Bengali. *What's happened?*

He replied, in English, "Nothing."

"*Amake ekhane anle keno?*" She screamed. *Why did you bring me here?*

"What do you mean? We're married. I love you." He replied.

"*Bar bar mithye kotha bolcho keno?*" She pleaded. *Why do you keep lying to me?*

"I'm not lying." He said.

Eventually she learnt to speak to him in English, in the tongue he had no trouble lying in. Perhaps it was because they had only learnt that tongue, not lived in it.

She burnt her wedding *sarees*, bought second-hand jeans from the Heart Foundation, cut and bleached her hair.

She learnt to say, "Fuck", "I Hate You" and "I know there's someone else."

She learnt to say, "I want a divorce."

They talked through the night, covering and recovering old ground like a tired If-Then-Else loop.

In the morning he left.

They ran into each other again, in that cheap little Indian restaurant off Princes Street, with the peeling stick-on Indian designs on the floors and windows.

He had the table nearest the kitchen; so close that the steam from the boiling pots clouded their glasses and singed their eyebrows. He was teaching Barra to eat rice with a spoon.

"Arka? *Kemon acho?*" she smiled. *How are you?*

She wore a loose *kurti* over worn blue jeans, gold hoops through her ears, long black hair streaked with red. She wore a tall smiling man on her arm.

"Smita! *Bhalo.*" Arka smiled back. *Good.*

"We saw you through the window, and came to say hi," Smita said.

"Come join us," Barra said, rising and pulling up two more chairs. "There's plenty of room."

She looked at them, took one, and sat down beside him.

Bengali Terms Used:
1. *Saree*: A long rectangular cloth that is draped and worn by women.
2. *Papad*: Thin disc shaped seasoned crepe, usually consumed fried or roasted
3. *Batik*: A method of block printing on cloth/A type of printed cloth
4. *Chanachur*: A spicy snack food mixture made of lentils, nuts, gram flour, etc.
5. *Alpana*: White patterns or paintings commonly created on religious or other auspicious occasions
6. *Kurti*: Short blouse

ANWESHA CHATTOPADHYAY is an Indian reader, writer, illustrator, editor, aspiring novelist, occasional playwright, and undercover wizard. She loves reading, sleep and travel. She is currently pursuing a Master's degree in English Literature from Jadavpur University, Kolkata and almost as eagerly pursuing elven war-criminals with her online gaming group.

Emily Rogers

Lost Mountain, Michigan

A bird lands on the wire and he asks me what kind it might be. I tell him
I do not know. They have been migrating. We are hiding under the bed
and there are white mountains outside the window. We discuss whether
it will rain.

Then I wake up.

There is a pain in my neck and I see a cobweb in the corner of the hotel
room as I open my eyes. It is summer and the breeze shakes the cobweb
but does not tear it. There is the sound of waves outside the window,
crashing somewhere on the lake's shore. I can see through the curtains
a family of pale white children in bright blue bathing suits running out
to the rocky shore. There are two girls, a mother, one boy, a father. The
girls all beautiful, the mother glamorous, the son unruly, the father lightly
fat, all as it should be. The door of my room opens and the maid and I
exchange a glance over pale yellow sheets, brown carpet, pastel watercolor
paintings, the smell of cigarettes. She pushes back her cart and closes the
door again.

I try to go back to sleep but my room is closer to the lake's shore than
I thought and I can hear the children giggling as if whispering in my ears.
Through the curtain their matching bathing suits are reflective in the sun.
Their mother holds a picnic basket, the father a red beach umbrella. All so

right. Their order in the morning sun makes my throat hurt and I grasp out for my cup of water on the nightstand, but cannot reach it.

It is 10 am in the summer. I have overslept and know it but do not mind too much. My stomach growls for barely cooked scrambled eggs, warm coffee, tight faux leather seats, for the faces of the men who drive through here with scarred beards and for their women, if they have women, with rose colored cheeks and palely yellow teeth.

The son yells mom and I hoist my body off the bed.

Next to the fogging glass of water is the half eaten cheeseburger from last night, the wrapper greasy. I toss it in the trash as I head to the bathroom, my feet brushing the brown carpet and not feeling a thing.

I pass all the photos that have collected on the desk. Me beside mountain after mountain after mountain. Not a single one right.

At the complimentary continental breakfast I take two plates of scrambled eggs. The yolks make me ravenous. I wonder if maybe there is something off about the eggs, something they've put in them that makes the bright yellow liquid so addictive. I'd been assuming that they were just undercooked, but now I realize I cannot place the yolk's taste. Either way I finish it quickly and sop up the puddles of yellow with my toast.

The old woman sits across the dining room, beside the large windows that look out onto the lake. I've decided we're friends though we've never spoken. Today she wears a sweater with a large tree on it, and a stream running next to it. In the crochet there are mountains in the distance.

Her lips are ashy pink and do not move. I do not know why she sits there with a full plate of eggs. I once sat the entire breakfast waiting for her to eat or to leave or to breathe. But she just sits in her booth by the window looking at nothing in particular until a bus boy tells her that breakfast is over. Then she gets up and looks at the postcards in the gift shop, turning each one in her hands but never buying any, until the restaurant reopens for lunch and she returns to her booth by the window. She's been doing this since I got here. We're comrades, I think.

I think I'll drive west today, around the lake, I haven't taken that road for a while. I'll take a new highway and see how long the battery on my camera lasts and try to get back at a reasonable hour. But these drives always lead me farther than I think, and when it's time to return to the hotel I find I'm miles away and the restaurant is always closed. I have to go to the nearest McDonald's for a hamburger, not that I'm really hungry, but I've always felt it's best to have dinner, even if it's merely ceremonial.

I've thought of befriending one of the truck drivers or businessmen who stay here. Maybe I could talk to them and get them to save me some dinner for when I get back real late. But their faces, as they eat their eggs, become frightening when they look in my direction. It's probably best not to go near them. Their facial hair looks more like a shadow wrapped around their jaws, shaggy and nightmarish, or if they're clean I think I can see the grease dripping from their black hair. And the women are out of the question. They would probably try to figure out about stuff. Make things complicated. Seem too curious. That's why I like the old lady; we can commune over breakfast across the room and not learn a single thing.

The dining room is hung with the same watercolors as the room, different scenes of creeks and fields. One shows a high peak, the trees are only tiny dots. I stare at it as I finish my coffee.

I drive west until 2 o'clock. There's nothing on the road that looks even moderately promising. West is all flat, I should have made a note of that, I should start keeping more meticulous notes. I stop at a convenience store off the highway and get a cup of coffee. I finger a composition notebook but decide to save my money. The cashier barely looks at me. But we exchange money easily so I seem to still be somewhat here.

As the $1.50 slips between us, I suddenly intensely materialize before her and my palms begin to sweat.

"Here's your change."

"Mhmmm."

"What're you doing round here?"

"Just, um, driving through."

"Nice, it's real shit around here, get out as fast as you can." Her laugh is light and girlish, and she fixes me with cat eyes and glossy lips. I hear my laugh come out raw, incorrect. I stare at her for a moment, wait for some more words to come from her feline mouth, before realizing I have dematerialized again and her eyes have gone flat.

"Thanks." I cup the change in my hands like a baby bird.

"Mhmmm."

I leave and the door behind me slams as if the glass has shattered, but I look back and find it completely intact. A cold wind blows under my shirt, and I try to see if there is any sloping up on the horizon, but there is no sign of mountains.

It began with the dreams.

Each night a fine carefree floating gives way to the image of a figure leading me by the hand up a mountain. I fall, lose my grasp, and then begin again. The figure waits, or sometimes leaves me. A flock of birds flies overhead. I notice them when I first fall. They are just the backdrop. But then I hear them turn violent; their wings hit each other, each bird eats at the other. They become some black mass, ever shifting, and I can just see that they are still birds by the spaces their moving bodies leave between each other.

We walk for hours then stop. On the mountaintop there is a house. The figure takes me in and sits me down at a table. Then the house sinks into the earth and fills with birds. Then I wake up. Sometimes the dreams are more violent, sometimes less. Sometimes the birds fly into my mouth. Sometimes the mountain is sunny. Sometimes it snows.

I don't remember when these first dreams came. But as they did things began to move, or disappear entirely. I noticed it changing while everyone else seemed to carry on. First it was just the birds. Outside, packing groceries into my car months ago, maybe the car I have now I can't remember, I notice that there seems to be more of them. I see them move in the sky above the parking lot, strange patterns I think. Then they stop, line up on the telephone wire all the way down the block.

My boss disappears overnight and is replaced by a woman with straight yellow hair. She says something inspiring about the work we do. As she talks her nose begins to bleed and no one says anything and she does not notice and I do not say anything and try to forget it. Everyone on the news at night seems to smile more. I stop watching the news. On my lunch break I think I see a woman levitating, red shoes just brushing the ground, only to look again and find her feet planted on the grass. I take note of that.

The dreams come more violent. I see the face of the figure but always forgot what he looks like the moment I wake. A man leads me; I remember that much, and he has begun discussing the weather and wearing a yellow raincoat. Usually I am silent but sometimes I can talk back. My words come out strange. He tells me soon summer will come and then the birds will break through the windows of our house.

I try to tell someone about the dreams, but everyone seems distracted. The news says there is some big war on. Sometimes I think I see explosions in the night sky. No one seems to notice. One night I drive for hours and then turn around and drive back. I cannot remember why.

And the mountain.

At work I let my pencil stray. I trace the mountain on every piece of paper. Then my hand gets used to the motion and I draw it on every surface. My house is littered with mountaintops. I do not read the newspaper, but use it to sketch the mountain. I buy paint for the walls. When I run out of surfaces I draw it on my own body and once it washes away I draw it again. I pour out the flour and trace it on my kitchen counter. I try to find it. The Internet reveals nothing, though by this time I know it in every season, could tell you it's cliffs, describe how you walk up it, where it hurt your legs, where the boulders are. Going down though, I know nothing about that.

One day my job disappears, or the office moves or I am fired. I could not tell, it made no difference. Sometimes my boss would lean over to speak to me and blood would trickle over her face. And birds would fly into the windows and shatter the glass. Sometimes they died. Sometimes they flew into the office and watched as everyone worked.

There is the question of insanity. There always is.

Then I dream the figure says come find me, and so I do.

The birds have calmed since. The dreams steadied but still come every night. I drive my car and stop at each mountain. None of them are right, but I take a photograph to remember, in case I am wrong. I always get a stranger to take it, I don't know why. Maybe so I know and can remind myself I am really here. I once felt so much more substantial.

At 4 o'clock it begins to rain. I'm on a new highway where there are only grey flat lands with bundles of trees growing in circles every few miles. I imagine they are talking to each other. Once in a while a car passes me, its lights on and driving in the opposite direction. The rain gets so thick I can barely see the road in front of me. I decide I am being silly. I should turn back. When the rain comes in here it comes hard, it might not stop until morning.

I think of finally making it in time for dinner at the hotel. I cannot remember if they serve eggs then too, but the hope that they might makes me want to turn around. I'm too nervous to make a U-turn. Even after months of driving on these long highways. I cannot remember if I was once a good driver. Instead I take an exit that seems to slope in the other direction. Back towards the lake, though I have lost it for the moment.

This road is all flat, all forest. I stroke my hair down and bite my nails. Sometimes at the end of the day a mountain will materialize and I will thank God and take a picture, though it is always wrong. But today is particularly flat, and I feel that the day has been particularly pointless, only long swaths of green fields and a solemn feeling of the land fading away. So I turn on the radio, something that used to terrify me in the bad, bad days when everything was not right. Things are still not right, but I find some old music and hope it won't terrify too much.

The road is all gravel and lets me drive slowly. My nails have grown long so I bite them off slowly and deliberately. They fall on my lap in satisfying crumbles. The rain lets up and I don't pay much attention to the road. The radio is filling the car with a song I once knew. There is a pain somewhere but I cannot find it.

My finger begins to bleed.

On rare occasions, under the quietest of circumstances, I let myself think there are no mountains to be found. Once the man in my dreams told me that the weather was just a mistake in our DNA. Maybe there is no quest. Maybe these are just echoes of some strange sentiment. Now lost.

Maybe it's all sanity.

The forest clears and I think I can see the lake now and can find my way back.

When I return it is night. The neon light above the hotel says vacancy in green letters and I see it long before the place comes into view. Dinner is still being served. There are eggs; there will always be eggs. But there's a strange feeling of change in me, like the disorder and all scary bits from before. I do not want the violent birds back. But I cannot help myself. Sometimes it must be stirred again, since it seems I cannot disappear completely.

I sit at the booth next to the window that looks out on the lake. There's an old woman sitting across the table. I use my voice and ask if I can sit next to her. She says yes. We eat and speak of all things seen and unseen, dreamed and undreamed. She tells me what birds mean.

Then I go to sleep and dream again.

EMILY ROGERS is a writer and poet. She is in her second year at Oberlin College in Ohio and is a native of New York.

Michelle Nicolaou

Working Class Nightsong

We listen to your speech,
your passionate spit
lands on my forehead,
a forecast of cloudy weather
with a chance of recession,
though the speed of your tongue
is almost as rapid as the rise
in unemployment
you don't seem to fit
in the part where,
though I work for you,
my bank account states
00.0 in the best case.
The minus sign screeches
in my ear when
I try to make
wooden benches comfortable
until the red and blue
chopper copper
shoves me along
to excuse his pay.
My only tragedy
on this street

is the thought
that once,
we had dreamed
without sticks prodding
at our neck.

Trade my soul in for paper
Banker, you wanker.

Performance poetry: On peace
Cyprus 2015

As two elbows point at me
like ready guns
at a point of threat,
baggage I never packed
crawls into my journal
as sleeveless words
weave disconnected worlds
into delicate design.
The kindred of war
marches out to
a new land
from a country broken
but this land of the free
shares in a familiar
despotic madness that

slyly flirts with foreign borders.
But the troop walks on,
diversely unified
and in my liberation, I find myself
shared,
willingly dissected to an unseen enemy
who shape shifting slowly
becomes my best friend.
Accustomed to silence
and solitude,
compromise becomes a life line
as bed duvets are no longer yours,
night escalates into a tug of war
reminiscently tracing back
to my identity, to your identity.
War- the nucleus of our history,
the moulder of our consciousness
into a fort of defence..
Conflict conceived from centuries
of cultivation, misinterpretation, misinformation
deliberate disorientation, scratching
our meadow coloured line
longer and wider.
We lived on the opposite sides
of an island we both called home,
with the same yellow weeds,
the same frothing waves,
the same parents praying
to different gods.
Now, in the same bed
our words reflect the pain
of our people who

inevitably we differentiate into
distinct democracies
that never existed.
Our bilingual whispers
recall the boulders
so tactfully placed by
voices saturated by power,
dripping in a self interest
that sculpted a future so tragic
the sky begged not to be ripped in two.
But while it was left intact,
it had a higher price to pay
for it became the sole observer
of everything else being slit in two.
It grew eyes that held the tears in
until cataclysmic outlets
bathed the dusty platform
of division.
Made the line clear again,
the wall tower over
our torn capital
 houses collapsed
and tenantless,
revel in purging sunshine.
But the grit remains
while the sky remembers
that man forgets compassion
when he himself is in pain,
abandonment replays
under closed eyelids
of an entire nation
gnawing into the marrow

yet not once remembering
that his neighbour
was forced to do the same
and it was his own doing.
Directly or indirectly
as that blame hovers,
sucks the life out
of my people
who I dare not differentiate,
anymore.
No, I am not
 an idealist
I know our cultural dents
I've mangled myself
around them.
The alienation
the incestuous political activity
the filth we carry in our banks
the underhand deals
that shake souls along with handshakes
that then turn
And bury us in an early grave.
I know the hatred,
the fear it's created from
the bigotry my sisters and brothers
drown in
the shame and guilt
so eloquently laced
with blasphemous pride
that embraces the selfish
and denounces the selfless
as traitors.

But I am a traitor,
if stitching and gluing
torn soil is
a spit worthy crime.
My enemy hugged me.
She brushed my hair,
covered me when I kicked
the sheets off my bed.
handed me a towel and
danced with me.
She covered my ears
from the erosive resentment
with her two hands
that are so like mine
and made me believe,
that in a country divided,
people united.

MICHELLE NICOLOAU is an eighteen year old student from Limassol, Cyprus. With poetry, Michelle rationalizes the status quo so as to draw out their divisions and oppressive consequences on society. Her poetic landscape amalgamates location and history with the human condition as to combine single narrations with a much wider context.

Sean Larney

Edinburgh/My Home Town

Edinburgh.
A place of winding streets with uneven roads and hilly pathways
Where it's too easy to trip and faceplant the pavement.
Where cars obey the traffic lights (well, just about!)
Kinda like my home town.

A place of temperamental weather: murky skies, sunny skies,
Showers and deluges, baking hot summer days and Baltic winters.
Sleet, snow, hailstones. Colder than an ice bath on a Puritan Sunday
morning,
Before the sun peeps cheekily from behind dissipating clouds.
Kinda like my home town.

A place where English and another language collide.
Scots, the forgotten younger brother, dimming cries for attention among
the sixty or seventy thousand that speak it still.
Despite the best efforts of Robertson and others.
Scot's Gaelic, different again; divide and conquer is the key.
'The sun never sets on the British empire.'
But it's English really. Not British.
The people are split along lingual lines,
Kinda like my home town.

Edinburgh.
Defined by political unrest.
The thrust for independence defeated yet again.
The fear of their own rule too much for the people.
At the end of the day, history's written by the winners.
Don't pretend it's not true.
Kinda like my home town.

Edinburgh.
With its crisp clean air full of whispered promise
For writers with talent and drive to succeed.
A city where writing and culture are revered
And great writers punch far above their weight.
Rowling, Pottering away, spawning a love of reading in world youth.
Doyle made several Holmes here, still adored by millions,
And Stevenson found his own Treasure Island.
A city of literary culture then.
Kinda like my home town.

Edinburgh.
A city packed with second hand book shops.
The places where different worlds meet,
Sweeping you into myriad worlds constructed by other minds.
'Culture with character,' my grandmother said.

Literary festivals coming out its ears,
Books celebrated to the point of insanity.
A Mecca for authors and readers alike
Kinda like my home town.

Edinburgh.
Where ceilidhs and trad music ring loud and true
As a vibrant culture is expressed in other ways than dying words.
Where many gather each year for a theatre festival world renowned
Yet remaining on the Fringe.
Where new playwrights and artists are welcomed into the limelight
And share in the fame desired by so many.
Kinda like my home town.

Edinburgh
A place where the night life is pubbing and clubbing
After rapturing readings by distinguished authors in carpeted rooms
dappled gold by the dipping sun.
A place where, despite your best efforts and your promises to your
stomach,
You give in and order Chinese food at two in the morning
Because of peer pressure from wonderful friends who live life in the
moment,
Though you wonder dubiously at the wisdom of eating anything from a
place named 'Hung Lam'.
Kinda like my home town.

Edinburgh.
A place that bridges the void between Hell and Heaven
For a student of literature
Because of a simple thing called 'baggage allowance.'
Forcing you to choose between clothes and books.
Kinda like my home town.

Edinburgh.
Where I met many inspirational people from the four corners of the
world,
Where I fell in love with the throbbing cultural heart of the city
And where I truly learned to live on my own.

Edinburgh.
Where I found my calling to write,
True friends, real life, good times, bad times.
Laughs, cries, independence.
The place where I learned how to live, for real.

Not like in my home town.

Germans and Jaffa Cakes

*The house of **Séamus Gilligan**, a man in his mid-forties. A rural but modern kitchen in the west of Ireland. Stage left is a door, with a couch next to it adorned with a floral pattern. A hearth, centre stage and towards the back, stands unlit. Stage right, **Séamus** sits at the kitchen table, nursing a cup of tea. Behind him is the kitchen counter, a sink and several cupboards at ground level. **Séamus** is stirring his tea and holding a Jaffa Cake, with the box open on the table. He can be heard muttering incoherently.*

*Enter **Barry**, a boy of sixteen, in a state of wild excitement.*

Barry: Séamus!

Séamus: (*startled, he drops the Jaffa Cake into his tea.*) What?!

Barry: Have you heard about these new lads that are building the new shopping centre?

Séamus: Barry, look now, you made me drop me biscuit into me tea.

Barry: Never mind that now. Did you not hear me say they're building a *shopping centre* up the road?

Séamus: 'Never mind that now', he says. Barry, d'you know that's a good ten cents getting soggy at the bottom of me tea? And I could choke on a crumb as well. … 'tis a feckin' lethal cup of tea now, Barry!

Barry: Séamus, will you shut up for a second and listen. They're building a shopping centre in Belmullet town.

Séamus: Sit down there and have some tea, and be saying ahead.

(**Barry** *sits down.* **Séamus** *pours him a cup of tea from a large pot on the table.*)

Séamus: A shopping centre? What're they selling?

Barry: Food it is they're doing mainly. There'll be a bread section, and a meat section, and a whole section for chocolate, and *another* for sweeties, imagine!

Séamus: It does sounds like 'tis a supermarket they're building, Barry.

Barry: Eh?

Séamus: A supermarket, it does sound like, and not a shopping centre at all.

Barry: There doesn't be a whole whack of difference between them two now Séamus, in fairness.

Séamus: There does be a good whack of difference between them two, Barry, and the main one would be that supermarkets is for food, but shopping centres is for all sorts. Are they selling clothes, did you hear?

Barry: They're not, now.

Séamus: Well, there you are so.

(*Pause.*)

Barry: (*to himself, thinking aloud.*) What is it they're called, now?

Séamus: Supermarkets, sure amn't I after saying?

Barry: Not that. 'Tis their name I'm onto now.

(*He thinks hard for a minute.*)

Barry: It does have 'lid' in the name, I know.

Séamus: Oh that's that one what's owned by the Germans.

Barry: Sure isn't everything owned by the Germans these days?

Séamus: Lidl it is they're called, I remember. Lots of Lidls do be around the place now.

Barry: Is it spreading they are?

Séamus: It is.

Barry: 'Tis like … opening the lid, and they all come out. A lid on a can of Lidls. A Lidl lid. ….

Séamus: (*after gaping at **Barry** aghast for a moment.*) Barry, sometimes I do wonder about getting your brain scanned, do you know that? To be seeing what's going on up there. Anyway, 'tis 'mushrooming' is the right word to be using in that context, and not be piling on the shite humour when I've been good enough to pour you that tea, now.

Barry: Ah, 'tis very unfair you are to me altogether Séamus.

(Pause.)

I do hope these Lidl fellas will be havin' Jaffa Cakes at their new store. Mad for the Jaffas, I am.

Séamus: The Jacobs ones.

Barry: Ay, the Jacobs ones.

Séamus: Jacobs is an Irish company now, Barry.

Barry: I did know that, Séamus. Sure 'twas always an Irish company.

Séamus: I'm only mentioning it because the Germans might not be wanting to sell the Irish products.

Barry: Ah, why not now?

Séamus: 'Tis business. Them Germans won't want to be sharing their euros with Irish companies. They might even be selling new German Jaffa cakes with a smaller orange bit. Germans is very practical altogether: they'll want to save on orange bits.

Barry: But the orange bit does be the best part!

Séamus: Sure the Germans don't give a freckled arse whether you think the orange bit is the best part. The Protestants now, they might …

Barry: *(distraught.)* Terrible news this is altogether!

Séamus: I did hear that Brída McBride was trying for a job as a cashier. It must be at this new Lidl, so. Is it opening soon, is it?

Barry: A month it is until the grand opening. They're having Dr. McSharry cut the ribbon since he's the best with sharp objects. We wouldn't want a repeat of Billybob Canty's neutering incident, like.

Séamus: Jaysis, we wouldn't, right enough. Horrible affair that, altogether.

(Pause.)

Barry: She'll never get it. Sure Brida has a face like a slapped testicle. All red and hairy …

Séamus: I'd be agreeing with you on that now, Barry, minding you don't be saying that in public, now.

Barry: I did know about the shopping cent- supermarket. 'Tisn't an eejit I am, Séamus.

(*Séamus looks at* **Barry**, *who is digging in his ear with a finger. While* **Séamus** *watches,* **Barry** *takes a key from his pocket and uses that instead.* **Séamus** *is about to say something, then lets it go.*)

Séamus: I did hear the rumour that Brida is going for the interview all the same. She might be able to be gettin' those German fellas to stock the Jacobs Jaffa Cakes, and not the McVitie's, or some German budget saver shite.

Barry: She probably looks like a female German is why.

Séamus: Is true, but she does have the ear of Michael Lafferty, and that's not all she does have.

Barry: Is it his willy you're sayin' she has as well? In her hairy hand, like? I wouldn't like that. 'Twould be like putting your willy in a gorilla's hand.

Séamus: No! That isn't what I was sayin' at all!

Barry: What so?

Séamus: (*caught out.*) Never you mind that now. Be eating your Jaffa Cakes there.

(*Pause.*)

Séamus: (*pensive.*) The female Germans are fierce hairy, all the same.

Barry: They've more hair than the men.

Séamus: They do, right enough.

Barry: What is it their leader is called again? Murky or something?

Séamus: Merkel, it is.

Barry: Right you are now. She looks like a shaved wolf.

Séamus: And they've that fella that's Pope. Benedict.

Barry: Yeah. He looks a bit like that evil fella from *Star Wars* with all the wrinkles. Darth Sidious. Darth Sidious is feckin' hairless in the films, except for his head.

(*Pause.*)

Barry: Are we having dinner soon Séamus? I want to be catching tonight's Big Big Movie. 'Tis *There's Something About Mary* this week. Ben Stiller does get his willy stuck in the zipper of his trousers.

Séamus: Like Billy Canty's was?

Barry: 'Tis exactly like Billy Canty's was, except they don't be showing the blood. Are we having dinner soon though?

Séamus: Go on in there and set up the film. Don't be touching any more of them Jaffas now, before having your dinner.

*(He gets up and pours the undrunk tea down the sink. As this is happening **Barry** picks up the Jaffa Cakes and sneaks out of the room. **Séamus** doesn't notice.)*

Lights down.

SEÁN LARNEY completed his master's degree in English at Trinity College Dublin in August 2015. Currently he works part time as a drama teacher in south Dublin. He writes whenever he can, and is motivated by the desire to make people laugh. His writing is fuelled by endless cups of tea.

www.ingramcontent.com/pod-product-compliance
Lightning Source LLC
Chambersburg PA
CBHW071345130626
46556CB00005B/2044